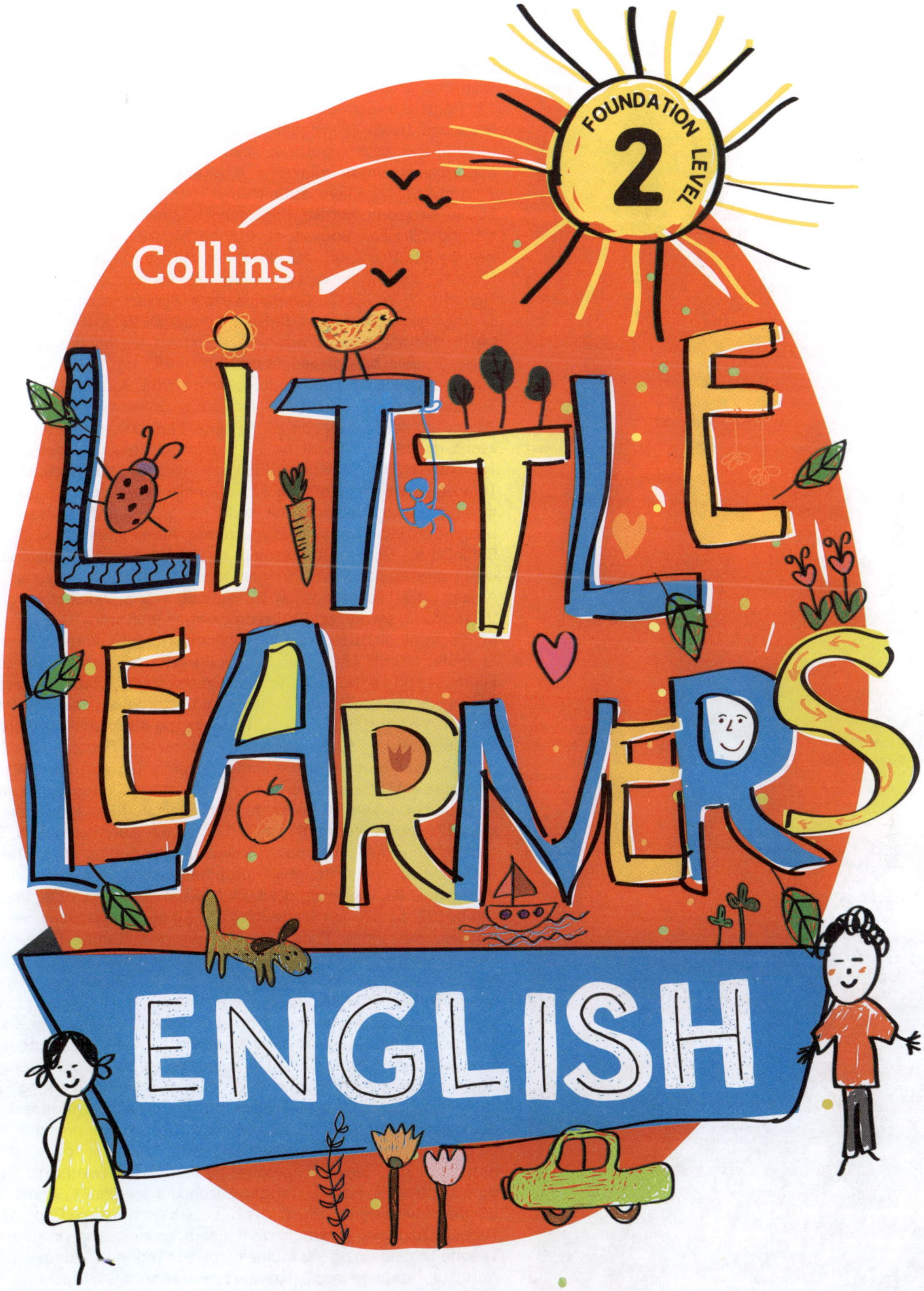

SERIES EDITOR: RANI T.

Published by Collins Learning
A division of HarperCollins*Publishers*
India Private Limited

HarperCollins Publishers
A-75, Sector 57, Noida,
Uttar Pradesh 201301, India

1 London Bridge Street, London, SE1 9GF,
United Kingdom

2 Bloor Street East, Toronto, Ontario M4W
1A8, Canada

Lvl 13, 201 Elizabeth Street (PO Box A565,
NSW, 1235), Sydney NSW 2000, Australia

195 Broadway, New York, NY 10007, USA

Browse the complete Collins catalogue at
www.collins.in
For any queries/feedback, please write to us
at **SCHOOLSUPPORT@harpercollins.co.in** or
call us on **0120-4044800**.

First published in 2020

Reprint: 10 9 8 7 6 5 4 3 2 1

ISBN: 978-935357-031-6

Artwork and layout by
Qualibre Creatives Pvt. Ltd.

Printed and bound by
MicroPrints (India), New Delhi

Acknowledgements

Cover: HarperCollins*PublishersIndia*

Title Page: HarperCollins*PublishersIndia*

Prelim Pages: radenmas, denkcreative, nonohana, graphic-bee

Inside: pg 8: StudioBarcelona, fireflamenco, Iuliia Kanivets, blueringmedia, Jirafic, nyamol, Vaibhav Designer, ogieurvil, Nikiteev_Konstantin, FARBAI, andegro4ka; pg 9: Tigatelu, drogatnev, luplupme, Toltemara, eliflamra, LeeDaniels, fireflamenco, S-S-S, dodo4466, Alfadanz, krishna pethani, Tigatelu, colematt; pg 10: nyamol, Nina_Piankova, Tetiana Lazunova, CandO_Designs, Redlio Designs, Hein Nouwens, blueringmedia, pleshko74, Tigatelu, nataka, denis_pc, clairevis, Vaibhav Designer, Mandryna, nyamol, Kauriana, graphic-bee, neyro2008, MariaTkach, johavel, grivina, AKARAKINGDOMS; pg 11: Tigatelu, blueringmedia, luplupme, Druzhinina, seamartini, drogatnev, dvarg, Tetiana Lazunova, Usagi-D, svaga, Nosyrevy, Tarchyshnik, Adi Wirawan, neyro2008, Alefclipart, natchapohn, krishna pethani, Tigatelu, colematt, igor170806, S-S-S, Redlio Designs, eduardrobert, Anastasiia_New, AKARAKINGDOMS; pg 14: bennyb, fireflamenco, Sonar512, 7romawka7, KanKhem, Yulia Melnyk, analia26, jagadeesha Gokhale, pg 15: Sonar512, StudioBarcelona, nataka, fireflamenco, 7romawka7; pg 16: graphic-bee, ogieurvil, KristinaVelickovic, Booka1, neyro2008, blueringmedia; pg 18: graphic-bee; pg 19: graphic-bee; pg 20: Alefclipart, Alfadanz, nyamol, Skathi, art-sonik, pijama61, Dar_ria; pg 22: Nikiteev_Konstantin, Vector, LeeDaniels, Tomacco, pijama61, Sudowoodo, Tigatelu; pg 23: Tigatelu; pg 24: Jirafic, CandO_Designs, Betsart, pleshko74, AntiMartina; pg 25: Jirafic, Skathi, Mykyta Dolmatov, Betsart, CandO_Designs, XXXX, pleshko74, ikryannikovgmailcom; pg 26: nyamol, Betsart, ogieurvil, KanKhem, hermandesign2015, Mandryna, luplupme, kbeis, graphic-bee, artvea, Mandryna, Jirafic; pg 27: CandO_Designs, Betsart, Sonar512, jagadeesha Gokhale, filo, bennyb, neyro2008, Booka1, Skathi, luplupme, nyamol, Tatiana Pankova, igor170806, incomible, art-sonik, Nikiteev_Konstantin, Tigatelu; pg 28: luplupme, sv-time; pg 29: sv-time, PerfectVectors, Yulyu, IconicBestiary, eliflamra, ksana-gribakina, FARBAI; pg 30: StudioBarcelona, nyamol, setory, eliflamra, ChrisGorgio, Tomacco; pg 31: blueringmedia, LeeDaniels, StudioBarcelona, setory, CandO_Designs, Tomacco, PerfectVectors; pg 32: ikryannikovgmailcom, Alefclipart, Usagi-D, Alena Igdeeva, Vector, VectorPocket, aldo_nat; pg 33: graphic-bee, fireflamenco, Jirafic, Usagi-D, ikryannikovgmailcom, nyamol, Alena Igdeeva; pg 34: AlfaSmart, Mochipet, RobinOlimb, Tigatelu, Druzhinina; pg 35: AlfaSmart, Druzhinina, RobinOlimb, graphic-bee, clairevis; pg 36: VectorMoon, Kittisak_Taramas, polygraphus, eliflamra, Naveed Anjum; pg 37: radenmas; pg 38: nyamol, S-S-S, Vidoslava, Parimal Pethani, dodo4466, VectorMoon, setory; pg 41: Dreamcreation, eliflamra, Usagi-D, Druzhinina, dodo4466; pg 42: VectorMoon, luplupme, VectorMoon, Tigatelu, Andrew_Rybalko; pg 43: fireflamenco, StudioBarcelona, LeeDaniels, StudioBarcelona, ikryannikovgmailcom, Mochipet; pg 44: pijama61; pg 46: Naddiya, Granell, Vectorpower, undefined undefined, eliflamra, Taisiia Iaremchuk, Alfadanz; pg 47: Naddiya, Vectorpower, StudioBarcelona, S-S-S, Parimal Pethani, polygraphus, Kittisak_Taramas; pg 48: krishna pethani, nataka, SIlviaCV, IconicBestiary; pg 50: blueringmedia, lemur4eg, Tigatelu, ONYXprj,primo-piano; pg 51: primo-piano, blueringmedia, Ennessy, lemur4eg, eliflamra, Alfadanz; pg 52: lishenjun, colematt, HitToon, eduardrobert, colematt; pg 54: luplupme, fireflamenco; pg 58: Armation74; pg 60: MariaTkach, vectorikart, FARBAI, Kauriana, Lanaclipart, schlol, saenal78; pg 61: pijama61, saenal78; pg 62: IconicBestiary, S-S-S, blueringmedia, colematt, -ELIKA-, Alefclipart, NiwatSingsamarn; pg 64: kontur-vid, pijama61, colematt, fireflamenco, Redlio Designs, luplupme, blondiegirl; pg 65: nyamol, colematt; pg 66: blueringmedia, colematt, aekikuis, MaksimYremenko, luplupme, hermandesign2015, rambo182; pg 67: hermandesign2015; pg 68: jehsomwang, Jenyk, eliflamra, Tarchyshnik, Naddiya, maradaisy, Photoplotnikov; pg 69: eliflamra, Jenyk, Evgeniya_m, jehsomwang, Photoplotnikov, Mochipet, blueringmedia, Tarchyshnik; pg 70: PerfectVectors, saenal78, Mykyta Dolmatov, MaksimYremenko, -ELIKA-, TDaria; pg 71: S-S-S, luplupme, Jenyk, blueringmedia, blondiegirl; pg 74: pijama61; pg 75: pijama61, TopVectorsl; pg 77: colematt; pg 78: neyro2008, Diane Labombarbe, Tetiana Lazunova, Iuliia Kanivets, Aaltazar, graphic-bee, Nikiteev_Konstantin; pg 79: Aaltazar, Iuliia Kanivets, Tetiana Lazunova, neyro2008, Diane Labombarbe; pg 80: Vaibhav Designer, Jenyk, denis_pc, Godruma, pijama61, ikryannikovgmailcom, Iuliia Kanivets; pg 82: Tetiana Lazunova, jagadeesha Gokhale, graphic-bee, blueringmedia, hermandesign2015, AndreyMakurin, dumayne; pg 84: Usagi-D, kathykonkle, luplupme, funnybank, dfli, eliflamra, LeeDaniels; pg 85: dfli, blueringmedia, Usagi-D, musri, luplupme; pg 86: drogatnev, pleshko74, blueringmedia, Hennadii, jperales; pg 88: Tetiana Lazunova, Tigatelu, Nosyrevy, luplupme; pg 89: colematt, nataka, Tetiana Lazunova, pleshko74, Tigatelu, luplupme, Nosyrevy; pg 90: Vaibhav Designer, musri, denis_pc, ONYXprj, Usagi-D; pg 91: kathykonkle, dumayne, Tetiana Lazunova, ikryannikovgmailcom, graphic-bee, drogatnev; pg 92: luplupme, Tetiana Lazunova; pg 93: ksuklein; pg 95: Tetiana Lazunova, jehsomwang, blueringmedia, Aaltazar, hardik pethani, pijama61, runLenarun, skalapendra; pg 97: adekvat, sldesign78, hermandesign2015, AndreyMakurin, Tomacco, Jiripravda, Tigatelu, Natalia, Darmoroz, rambo182; pg 101: KanKhem, bortonia, Ihor Kashurin, ONYXprj, Anastasiia_New, Diane Labombarbe, TopVectors, Shendart; pg 103: fitie, Tigatelu, Redlio Designs, Tetiana Lazunova, FARBAI, Darumo, incomible, Yulia Ogneva, drical; pg 107: Tomacco, Nina_Piankova, adekvat, Yulia Melnyk, lumpynoodles, seamartini, luplupme, MariaTkach, JuliarStudio; pg 108: yayayoyo, nidwlw, MariaTkach, Jiripravda, filo, IconicBestiary, nidwlw, Jiripravda, Tomacco, pleshko74; pg 109: melissahelddesigns, AnvilArtworks; pg 111: Anastasiia_New, Yulia Melnyk, Jiripravda, art-sonik, incomible, rambo182; pg 113: Jirafic, Skathi, Mykyta Dolmatov, Betsart, CandO_Designs, pleshko74, ambassador806, luplupme, kbeis, graphic-bee, artvea, Mandryna, blueringmedia, LeeDaniels, StudioBarcelona, setory, CandO_Designs, Tomacco, PerfectVectors.

Preface

Collins Little Learners, comprising 20 books in all, provides graded, age-appropriate learning opportunities targeting holistic skill development for children in the age group of 3 years to 6 years. Spread across three levels, the series spans **English**, **Maths**, **General Awareness**, **Art and Craft** and **Hindi**. The series comes bundled with a **workbook** for English and a book of **rhymes and stories** for each level. The books use a combination of hands-on activities, frequent recapitulation and child-friendly artwork to facilitate learning.

The early years are the most significant years for growth, development and learning. During this period, children need adequate opportunities for stimulating experiences as these favourably affect various learning abilities. Learning experiences, when chosen and planned properly, fuel the innate curiosity of children, and stimulate their thought processes.

Learning and Development During the Early Years

The goal of learning during the early years is to enhance the all-round development of personality and to inculcate healthy attitudes, life skills and good values. Creative play, well thought-out games and developmentally appropriate activities help children develop the necessary skills to achieve these goals. The skills that children need to acquire can broadly be categorized as:

Motor: Motor skills pertain not only to gross motor activities like walking and jumping but also include fine motor activities like the ability to hold a pencil and write. The development of motor skills is facilitated through several graded activities.

Personal, Social and Emotional: Personal, social and emotional development, necessary for the overall personality development of children, is achieved using a combination of hands-on activities, role plays, and thought-provoking stories and rhymes.

Linguistic: The ability to listen, speak, read and write is critical to success in formal learning environments.

Mathematical: The development of mathematical ideas and concepts is important at this stage since children will continue to build on this learning for most of their years of schooling.

Knowledge and Understanding of the World: This is achieved through activities that enable children to explore their surroundings at home and in the school, and interact with the people that they see around them.

Health and Safety: The idea of health and safety is introduced through activities, stories and retelling of real-life experiences to encourage children to focus on health and well-being.

Creative: Creative skills are developed through a host of activities involving art, craft, painting, roleplays, etc.

Logical and Rational Thinking: Activities that involve simple puzzles, pattern-completion and visual discrimination help children develop logical and rational thinking skills.

The Collins Little Learners Teacher Support Materials

The series includes extensive teacher support in the form of:

Teacher's Resource Books: Comprises stories, activity banks, classroom management and assessment guidelines

Multimedia eBook: Consists of animations, audio, video, slide shows, and interactive exercises

Print-ready Worksheets: Additional worksheets for practice and reinforcement, present in the digital support

Digital Flashcards: Flashcards with embedded sounds and animations for letter formation and letter-sound association

Animations and Songs: Animated stories and rhymes set to tune

Interactive Games: Interactivities to reinforce concepts in a fun and engaging manner

A note on the activity banks (included in the Teacher's Manuals)

The activity banks comprise hands-on activities that will help children develop the requisite skills to attain age-appropriate learning goals. In keeping with Howard Gardener's theory of multiple intelligences, the activity banks include options and variations that enable teachers to provide a planned cycle of experiences and opportunities, which foster each type of intelligence, to every child in their classrooms. The activity banks equip teachers to use the strengths of children as a means of complementing their less developed areas by valuing and nurturing the inherent abilities of the children.

Contents

Walkthrough

Two-page spreads used to introduce letters. The emphasis is on developing letter–sound association and supporting vocabulary development through a variety of exercises. The teacher's manual includes stories, which can be used to accomplish these goals.

Both upper case and lower case letters shown with pattern-tracing to facilitate identification and recognition

Exercise to reinforce letter-sound association and support vocabulary development

Simple action rhymes used to introduce little learners to language patterns such as rhythm, rhyme and alliteration. Affords opportunities for psychomotor development

Pattern-based writing of upper case letters

Simple revision exercises to reinforce concepts

Mixed revision activities enable teachers to assess level of learning and recall without a formal assessment

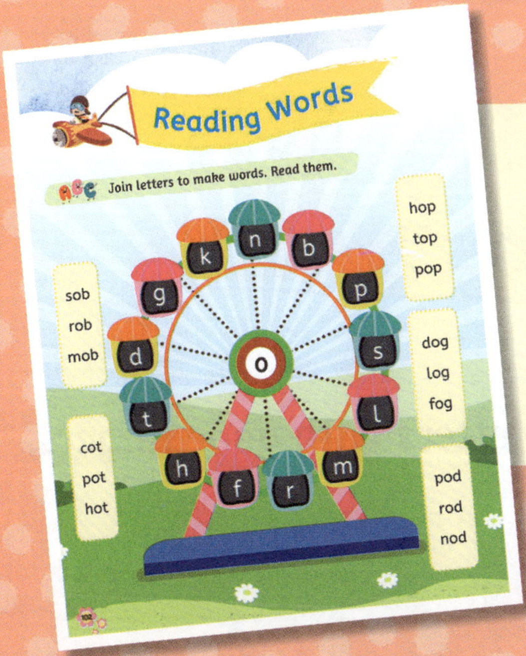

CVC words based on short vowel sounds introduced at the end of the book. Pages designed to encourage building and reading words through a simple game, either individually or in small groups.

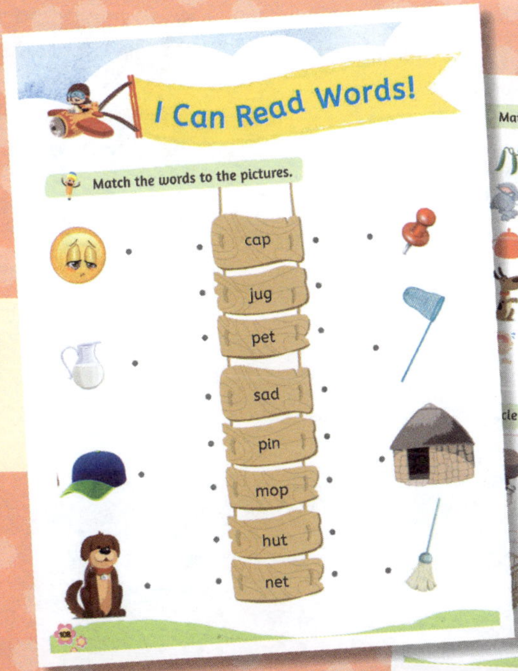

Revision pages help develop reading skills further

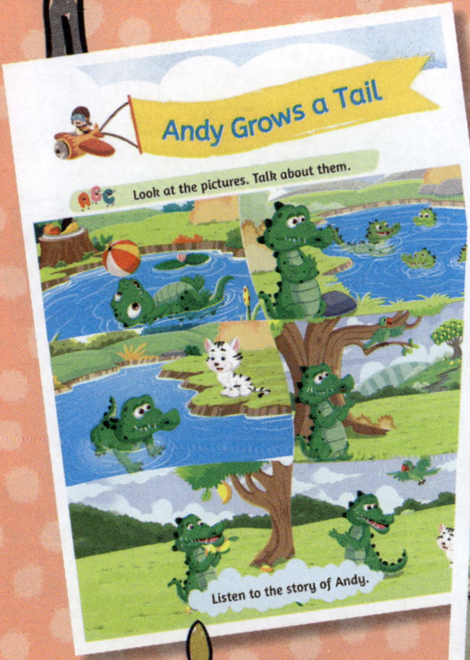

Interesting stories to introduce good manners, life skills, etc. and further language acquisition

I Know Aa-Zz

Say the letter names. Trace the letters with your fingers.

Aa

Bb

Cc

Dd

Ee

Ff

Gg

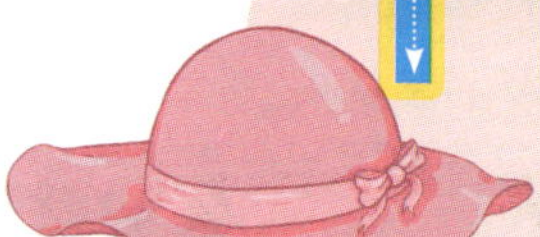
Hh

Ii

Jj

Kk

Ll

Mm

Nn

Oo

Pp

Qq

Rr

Ss

Tt

Uu

Vv

Ww

Xx

Yy

Zz

I Know Letter Sounds

Sing the phonic song.

The ant wants an apple /a/-/a/-/a/
The bug wants a ball /b/-/b/-/b/
The cat wants a candy /k/-/k/-/k/
The dog wants a doll /d/-/d/-/d/
I know the letter sounds, yes I do
I know the letter sounds, how about you?

The elephant wants an engine /e/-/e/-/e/
The fox wants a flower /f/-/f/-/f/
The goat wants a guitar /g/-/g/-/g/
The hen wants a hat /h/-/h/-/h/
I know the letter sounds, yes I do
I know the letter sounds, how about you?

The insect wants an igloo /i/-/i/-/i/
The jackal wants a jug /j/-/j/-/j/
The kangaroo wants a kite /k/-/k/-/k/
The lion wants a lollipop /l/-/l/-/l/
I know the letter sounds, yes I do
I know the letter sounds, how about you?

The monkey wants a mat /m/-/m/-/m/
The nightingale wants a nut /n/-/n/-/n/
The ostrich wants an orange /o/-/o/-/o/
The parrot wants a pen /p/-/p/-/p/
I know the letter sounds, yes I do
I know the letter sounds, how about you?

The queen wants a quilt /kw/-/kw/-/kw/
The rabbit wants a rocket /r/-/r/-/r/
The snake wants the sun /s/-/s/-/s/
The tiger wants a table /t/-/t/-/t/
I know the letter sounds, yes I do
I know the letter sounds, how about you?

The uncle wants an umbrella /u/-/u/-/u/
The vulture wants a vase /v/-/v/-/v/
The x-ray is in the box /ks/-/ks/-/ks/
The yak wants a yo-yo /y/-/y/-/y/
The zebra wants a zip /z/-/z/-/z/
I know the letter sounds, yes I do
I know the letter sounds, how about you?

Picture Reading

Look at the picture. Talk about it.

Spot the Difference

Spot 5 differences between the two pictures.

Hello Letter Tt

Trace with your finger. Name the pictures.

tree

turtle

tap

tomato

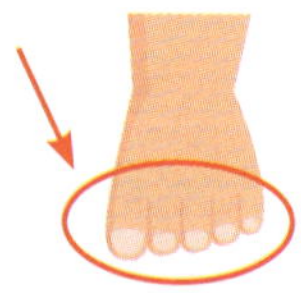

toes

teapot

train

tiger

Circle the pictures that begin with T.

tap

apple

fox

turtle

tomato

Trace and write.

T

SING ALONG

Tiny tiger shining
in the light!

Let me see you
jump to the right,

Now to the left
and again to
the right.

Tiny tiger shining
bright!

Hello Letter Ii

Trace with your finger. Name the pictures.

insect

inkpot

ink

India

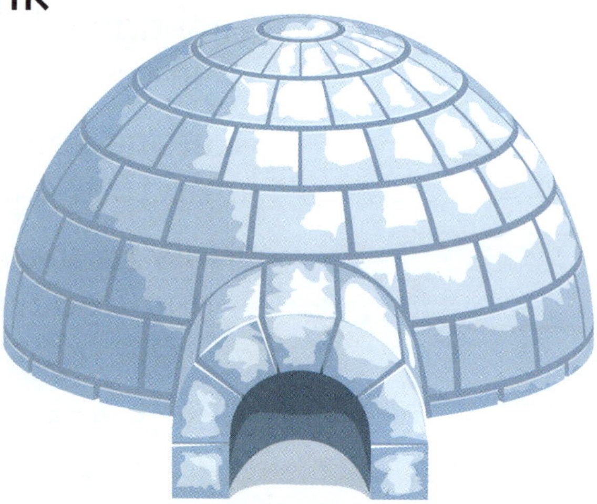

igloo

ill

Colour the insect. Take it to the igloo.

Trace and write.

I I I

I I I

SING ALONG

Incy wincy insect
climbing up the spout,

Down came the rain
and washed the
insect out.

Out came the sun and
dried up the rain,

Incy wincy insect
started climbing
up again.

Hello Letter Ll

Trace with your finger. Name the pictures.

leaf

Ll

lollipop

lamp

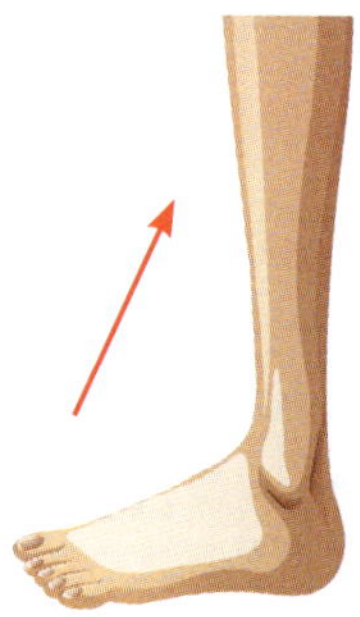

leg

lights

lion

log

Circle the pictures that begin with L.

lollipop

net

lion

kangaroo

lamp

Trace and write.

L

SING ALONG

Lenny lion jumps
up and down,
shaking his
mane about.

He throws his
arms into the
air, dancing
away without
a care.

Hello Letter Ff

Trace with your finger. Name the pictures.

flower

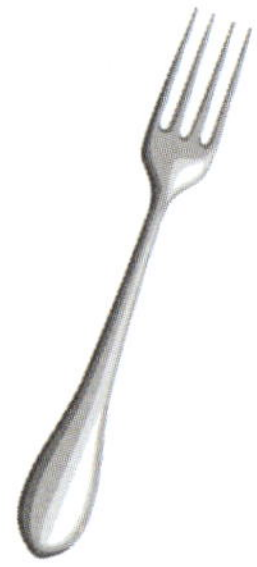

fork

frog

fire

fan

friends

fish

Colour the fish with the letter F. Use any colour that you like.

Trace and write.

F

SING ALONG

Fitzy frog hops
here and there,

Looking for food
everywhere.

Hop to the front
and hop to
the side.

Fitzy frog never
does hide.

Hello Letter Hh

Trace with your finger. Name the pictures.

hat

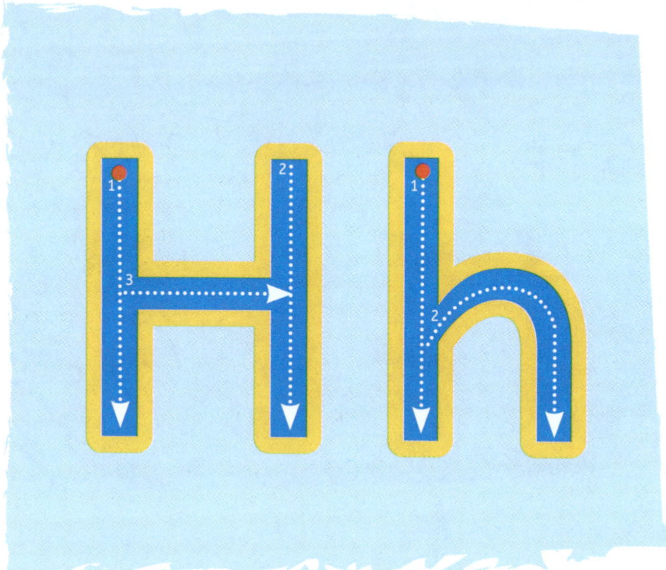

hot

horse

hut

happy

house

hen

Help Hettie the hen reach home by colouring the stones with H.

Trace and write.

SING ALONG

Cluck-cluck, cluck-cluck,
Hettie hen flaps
her wings!

Cluck-cluck, cluck-cluck,
Loudly Hettie hen sings.

Cluck-cluck, cluck-cluck,
See my new hat bright
and green.

Cluck-cluck, cluck-cluck,
This is the best hat I've
ever seen.

Hello Letter Ee

Trace with your finger. Name the pictures.

egg

envelope

eggplant

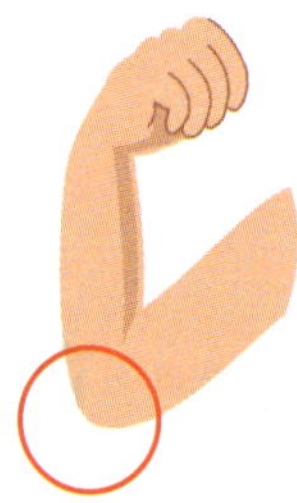

elbow

engine

elephant

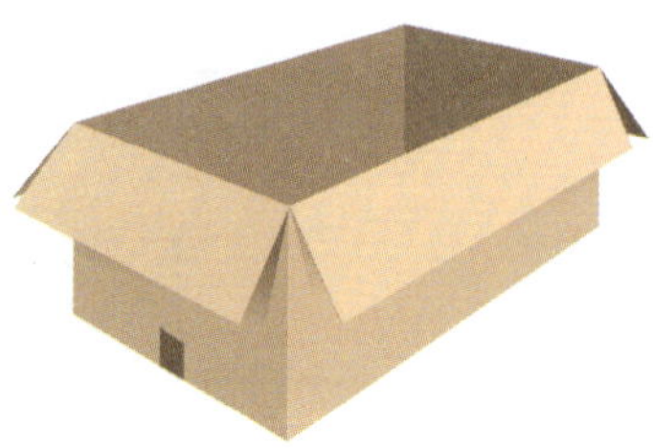

empty

Paste stickers of pictures that start with E.

Trace and write.

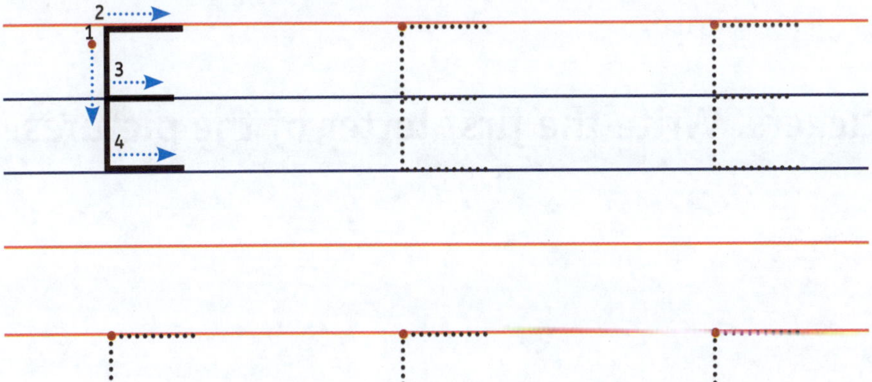

SING ALONG

Ellie elephant
has a long nose,
Ellie's nose
touches her toes.

Oh, my! What a
long nose! I have
to bend to touch
my toes.

I Know!

Name the pictures. Tick (✓) the correct letter.

E H F

T I E

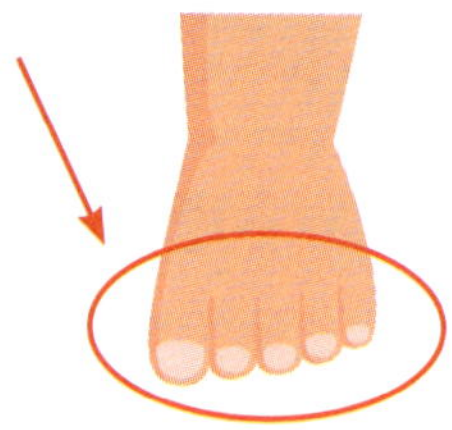

I L T

F H I

T F E

H F L

Paste the correct stickers. Write the first letter of the pictures.

Cross (×) the odd one out.

E 

T 

I 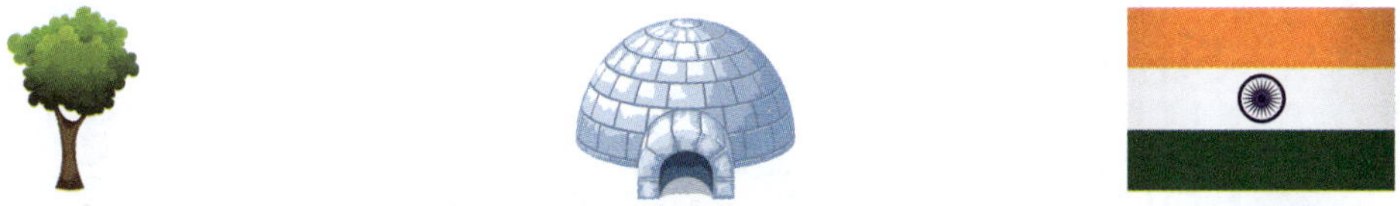

F 

L 

H 

Write the matching capital letter next to each letter.

f ______ e ______ i ______

l ______ t ______ h ______

So Many Things to See

Sing.

Look around, look around
So many things to be found
Some are near like this bear
Some are far like that car

Point out objects in the classroom and continue.

This table, that flag
This chair, that bag
So many things around me
So many things for me to see

Look at the pictures. Tick (✓) the correct word.

this that

this that

this that

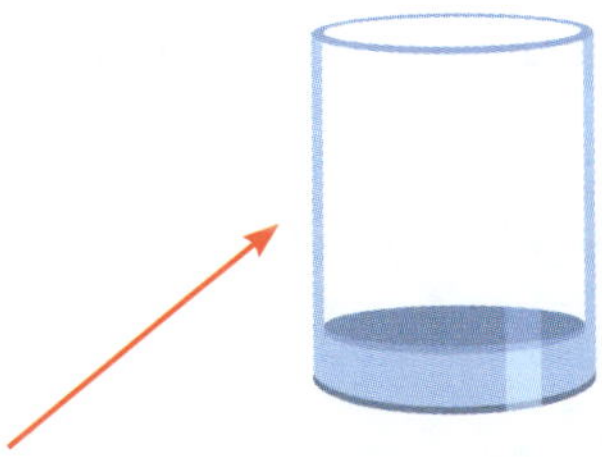

this that

this that

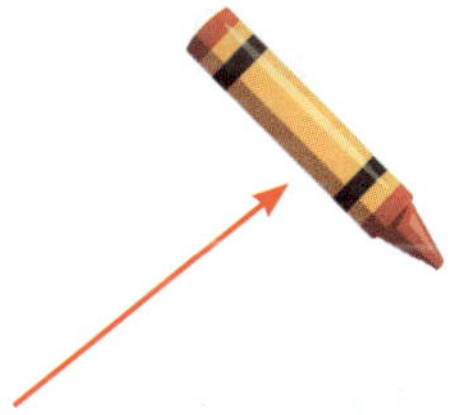

this that

Hello Letter Aa

Trace with your finger. Name the pictures.

apple

ant

axe

alligator

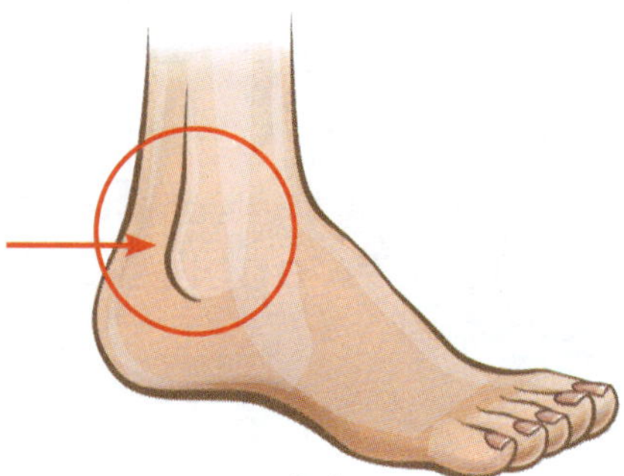

ankle

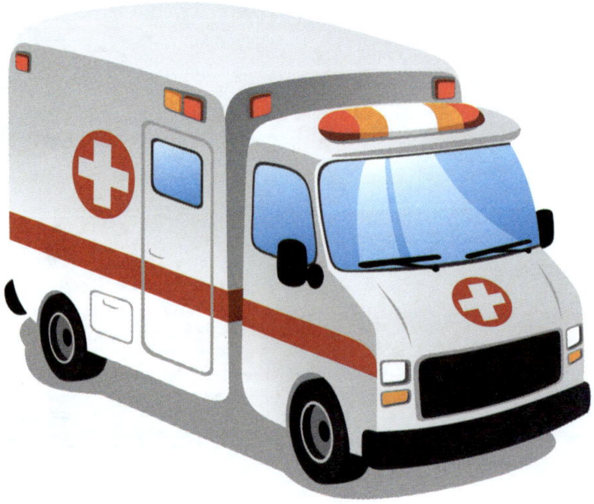

ambulance

angry

Paste the stickers of the images that start with A.

Trace and write.

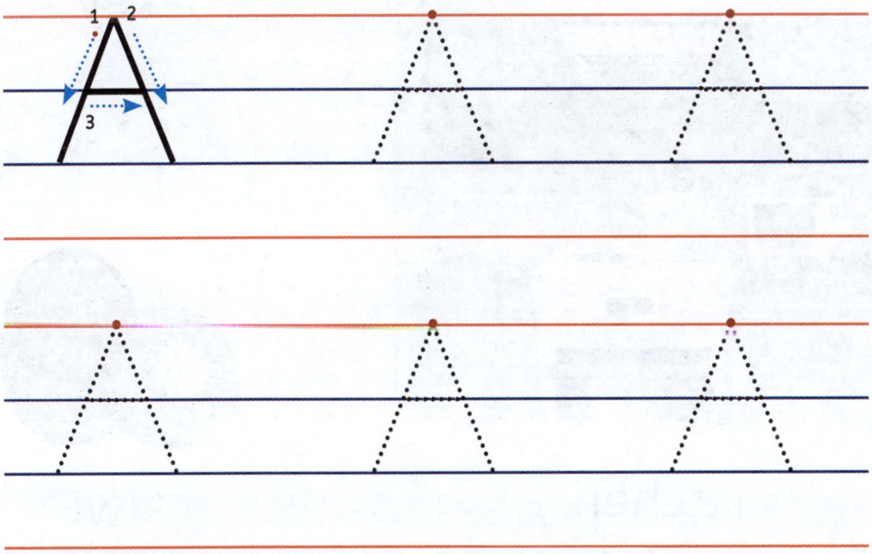

SING ALONG

Andy alligator jumps
up and down,

Thump, thump,
thump on the
ground.

Andy loves apples
juicy and sweet,

Chomp, chomp,
chomp Andy eats.

Hello Letter Kk

Trace with your finger. Name the pictures.

kite

king

Kk

kangaroo

key

kitchen

kettle

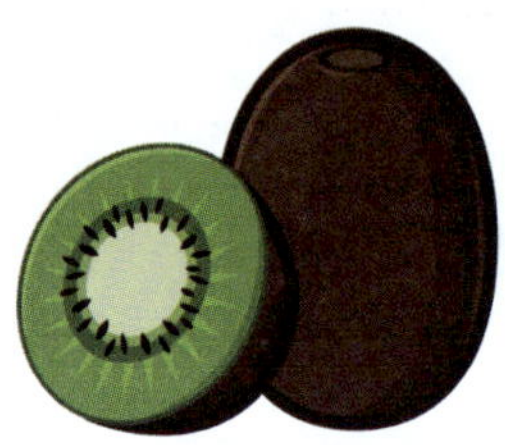

kiwi

Circle the pictures that begin with K.

net

lion

tortoise

egg

kangaroo

kite

frog

key

kettle

Trace and write.

K

SING ALONG

Kylie kangaroo
blows on her horn,
Kylie kangaroo
jumps on and on.
Kylie kangaroo never
does stop,
Till Kylie kangaroo is
right at the top.

Hello Letter Mm

Trace with your finger. Name the pictures.

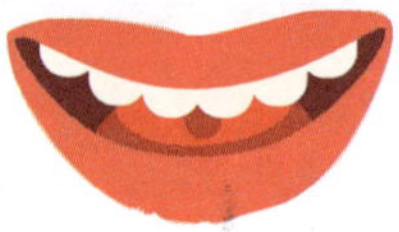

mouth

mango

moon

mug

monkey

mat

Help Monu by matching the pictures that begin with M.

Trace and write.

SING ALONG

Monu monkey is
a hungry fellow

He loves bananas
ripe and yellow

Hanging from the
tree by his tail

Monu eats bananas
without fail.

Hello Letter Nn

Trace with your finger. Name the pictures.

net

nurse

nest

nine

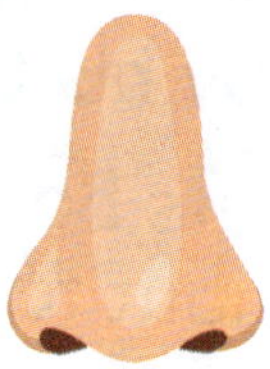

nose

night

nightingale

nib

Colour the leaves with the letter N green.

Trace and write.

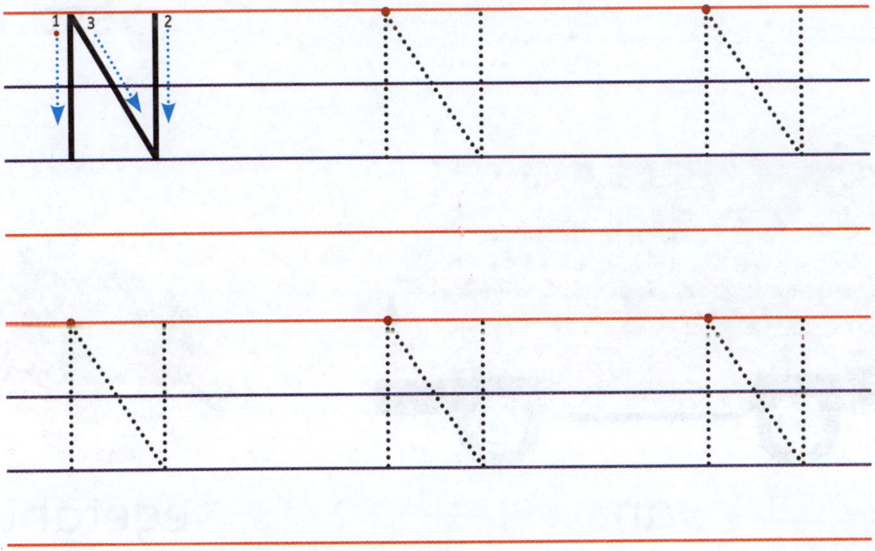

N

SING ALONG

Nyla nightingale
flaps her wings
Up and down as
she sings.
Nyla nightingale
lifts her wings
up high
As she flies in
the sky.

Hello Letter Vv

Trace with your finger. Name the pictures.

vulture

vase

vine

vest

violin

van

vegetable

Join the dots to complete the vase. Colour the picture.

Trace and write.

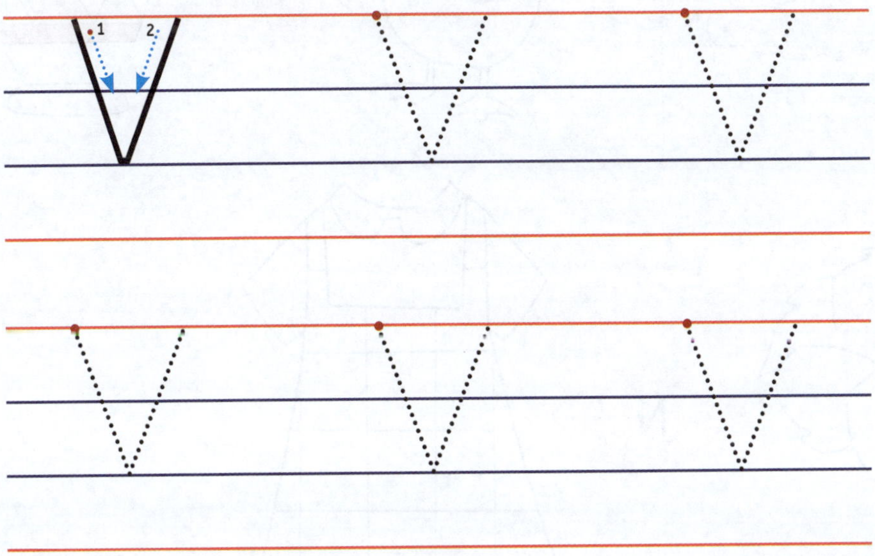

SING ALONG

Volly vulture is
hungry for
a meal.

He flies high and
low, looking for
a teal.

If you see him,
look down
and kneel.

I Know!

Thumbprint the correct pictures. Colour the other pictures.

A

K

M

V

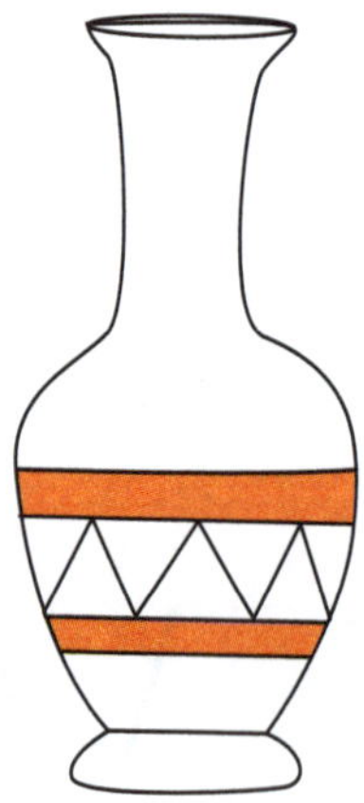

N

Tick (✓) the correct letter.

A K M

K L T

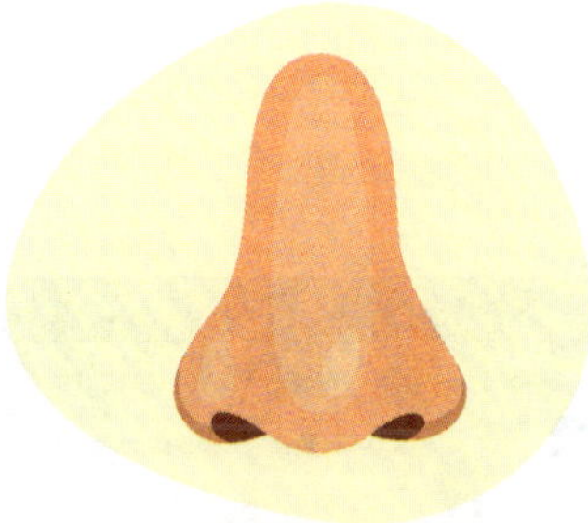

H F N

F M I

K V M

Write the matching capital letter.

a ______

k ______

m ______

n ______

v ______

Write the beginning letter of the picture.

Paste cotton to make clouds. Colour the letters that match the picture in each cloud.

K

N

M

A

V

M

Rita and Her Friends

Hello! **I** am Rita.
These are my friends.

This is Sandy. **She** loves to play games on her .

We go to school in the same .

This is Alex. **He** loves to play with his , Boxer.

We have a lot of fun in .

I she he we

Colour the pictures. Tick (✓) the correct word for each picture.

he she I

he she I

Paste your picture here

he she I

Hello Letter Ww

Trace with your finger. Name the pictures.

web

wall

watch

walrus

water

whale

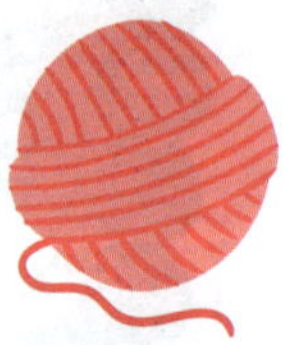

wool

Cross (×) the pictures that do not begin with W.

Trace and write.

W W W

W W W

W

SING ALONG

When you wake up, sing this song.

When you wake up, dance along.

Tap your feet all day long,

Walk, run, play and be strong.

Hello Letter Xx

Trace with your finger. Name the pictures.

X-ray

fox

box

X-mas tree

Trace and colour the X-mas tree.

Trace and write.

SING ALONG

This is an X-ray,
do you see?

It is a picture
of the bones
inside me.

See how big and
strong they be.

This is an X-ray,
do you see?

Hello Letter Yy

Trace with your finger. Name the pictures.

yo-yo

yellow

yak

yoga

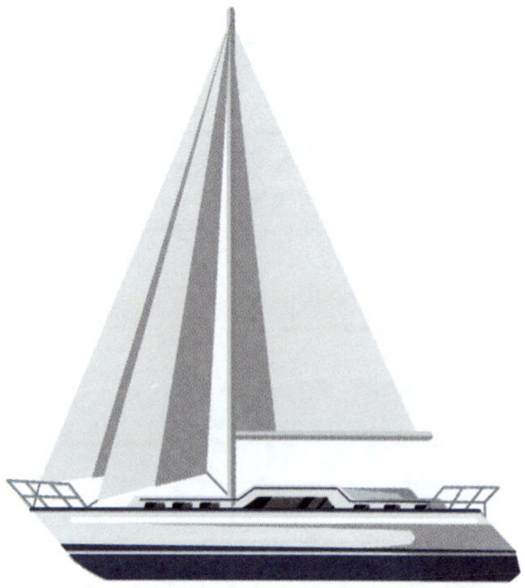

yacht

Match the correct pictures to Y.

Trace and write.

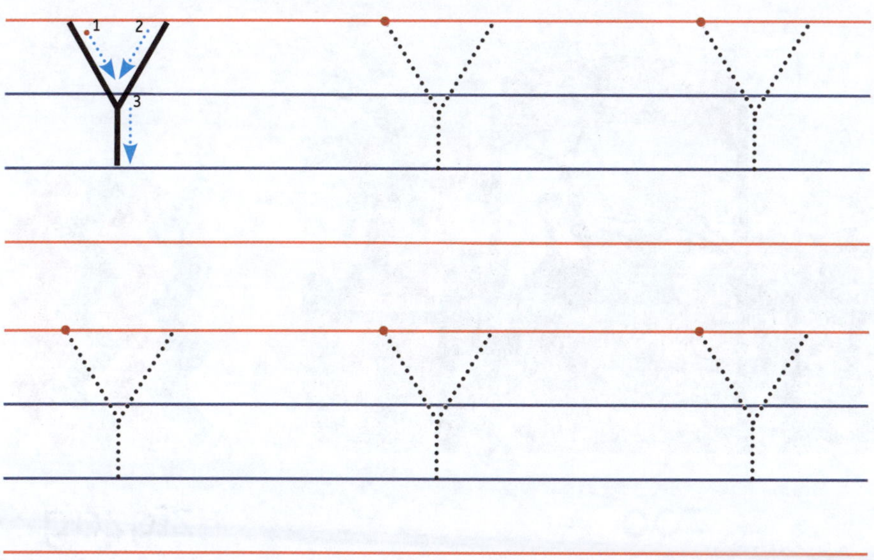

SING ALONG

Yellow yo-yo swinging
up and down,

Yellow yo-yo going
round and round,

Yellow yo-yo never
touching the ground,

Yellow yo-yo swinging
up and down.

Hello Letter Zz

Trace with your finger. Name the pictures.

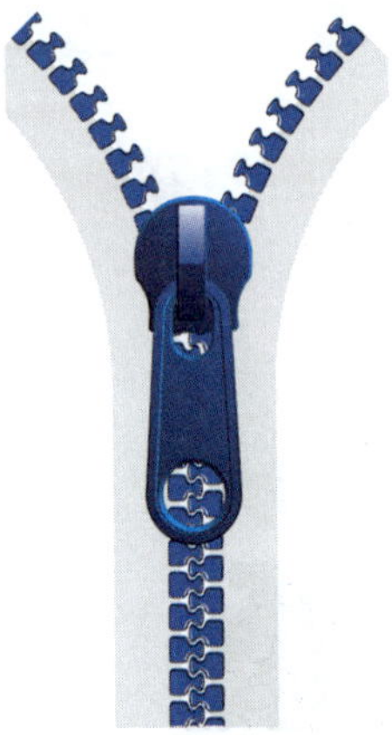

zip

zebra

zero

zoo

zigzag

Complete the stripes on the zebra. Colour the picture.

Trace and write.

SING ALONG

Zilly zebra has stripes black and white.

Zilly zebra goes left and goes right.

Zilly zebra walks in a zigzag.

Zilly zebra does not lag.

I Can Write!

Trace and write.

A K V

N M F

E I L

T H W

X Y Z

I Know!

Draw pictures with the given letters.

W

X

Y

Z

Colour the pictures. Cross (×) the odd one out.

W

X

Y

Z

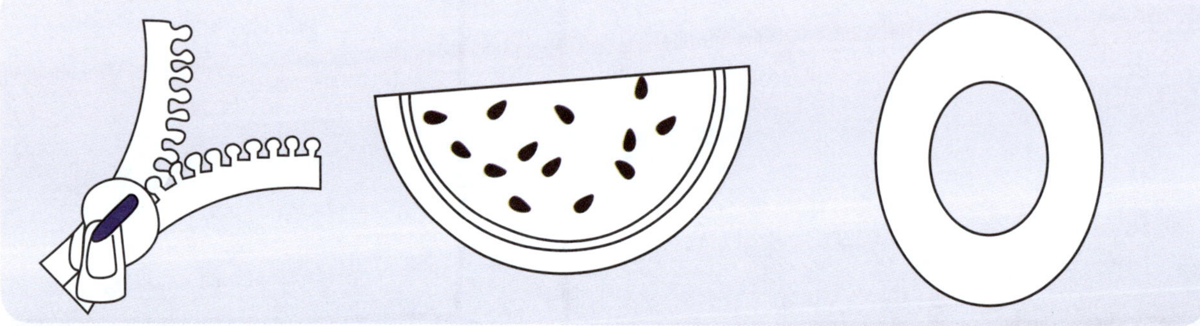

Print with cotton buds to complete the pictures.
Circle the beginning letter.

K

W

V

X

Y

W

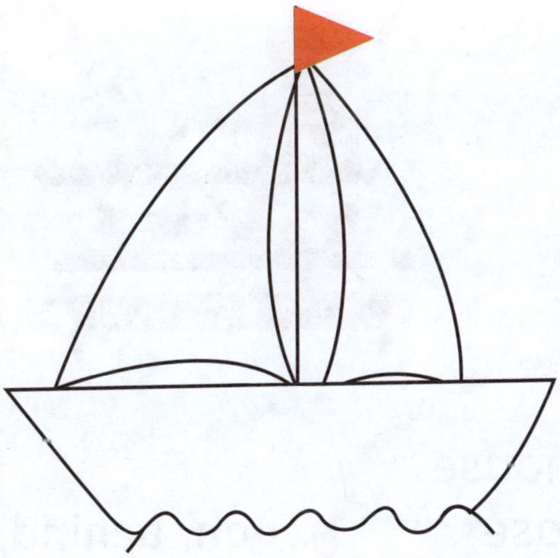

Y

Z

W

W

V

Z

Where Is My Cheese?

Sing.

The little grey mouse
ran here and there,
Looking for his cheese
everywhere,

On the table, behind
the teacup,

Between the plates,
inside the milk jug.

On the
shelf above
the table,

Under the chair,
beside the rug.

The little grey mouse
said, 'Pretty please,
Will you tell me where
is my cheese?'

on, behind, between, inside, above, beside, under

Match the pictures to the words.

inside

beside

behind

on

between

under

Hello Letter Jj

Trace with your finger. Name the pictures.

jug

jacket

jam

jackal

joker

jeep

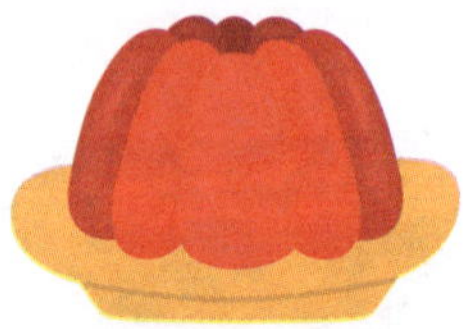

jelly

Help Jim find his jelly.

Trace and write.

J

SING ALONG

Jack the jackal
dances in the jungle,

Dances under the
sun and in the rain.

Jack the jackal
dances in the jungle,

Jack the jackal feels
no pain.

Hello Letter Uu

Trace with your finger. Name the pictures.

urn

up

under

umpire

umbrella

uncle

unhappy

Colour the umbrella. Paste stickers of raindrops.

Trace and write.

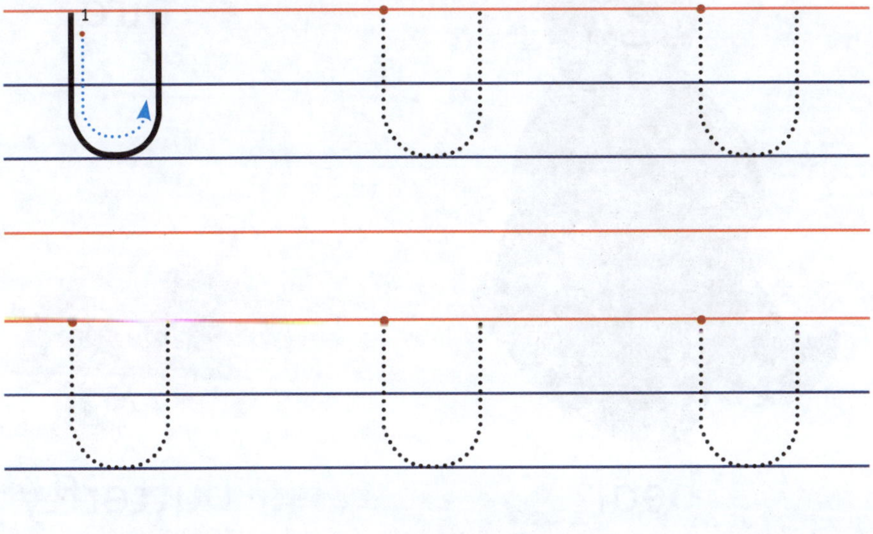

SING ALONG

My little umbrella,
bright and gay,

Come with me in
the rain to play.

I will hide you
when the rain goes
away.

My little umbrella,
bright and gay.

Hello Letter Bb

Trace with your finger. Name the pictures.

bat

boy

boat

bird

bear

ball

butterfly

Trace the patterns to take Betty bee to the hive.

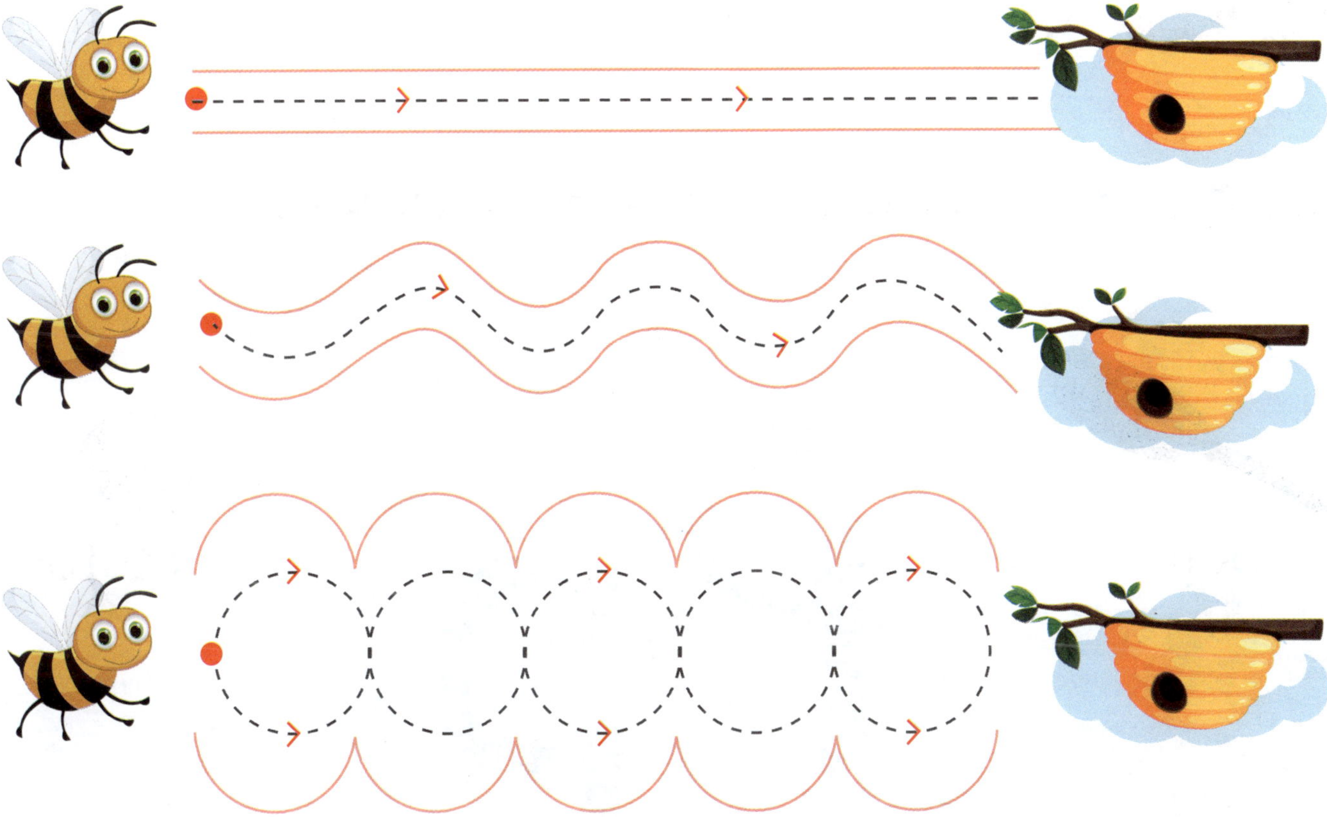

Trace and write.

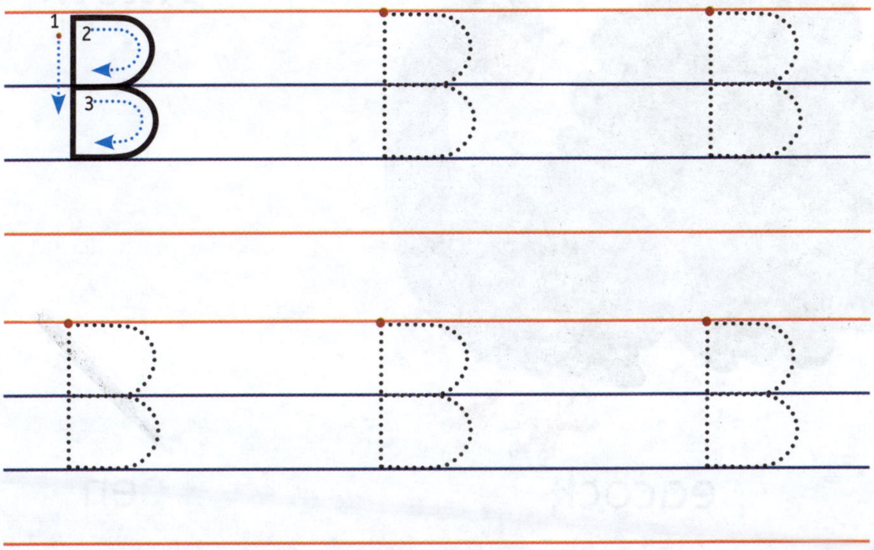

B

SING ALONG

Butterfly, butterfly
flutter around.

Butterfly, butterfly
touch the ground.

Butterfly, butterfly
reach the sky.

Butterfly, butterfly
say goodbye.

Hello Letter Pp

Trace with your finger. Name the pictures.

pan

potato

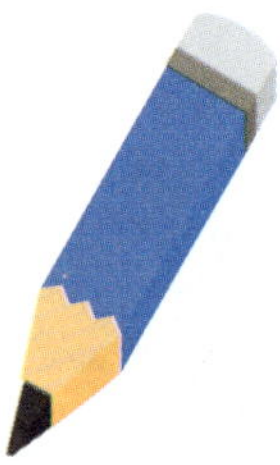

pencil

pillow

parrot

peacock

pen

Complete the peacock. Colour its feathers in blue and green.

Trace and write.

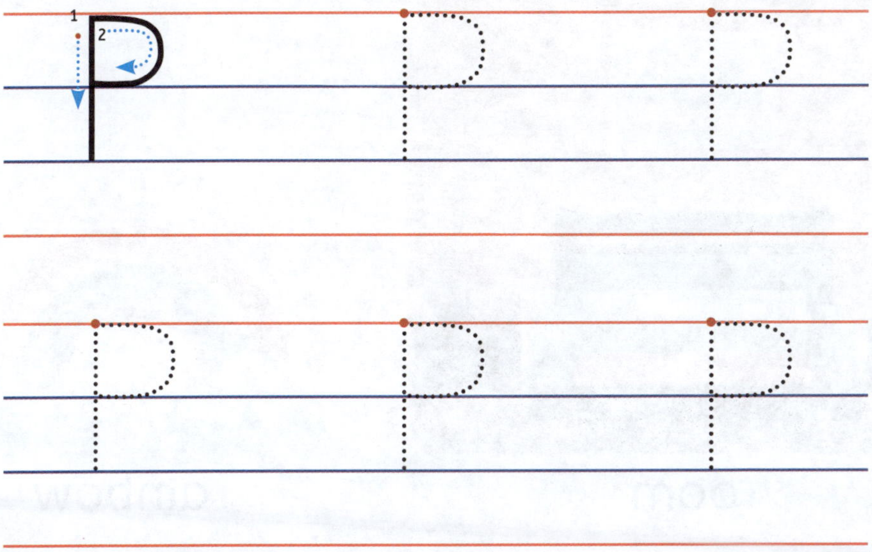

P

SING ALONG

Pretty peacock
dancing in the rain,

Spread your feathers
once again.

Pretty peacock will
you please

Dance some more
just for me?

Hello Letter Rr

Trace with your finger. Name the pictures.

rat

ring

rabbit

rocket

rose

room

rainbow

Cross (×) the odd one out.

Trace and write.

R R R

R R R

SING ALONG

Ruby rabbit lives
in a hutch.

Ruby eats carrots
for lunch,

She goes
munch-munch

With a loud crunch

Crunch-crunch
Crunch-crunch.

I Know!

Paste the wheels with correct stickers of capital and small letters.

Write the beginning letter of the pictures.

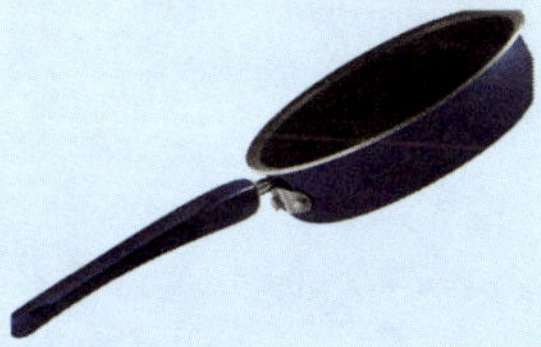

Tear and paste waste paper to complete the pictures. Write the beginning letter.

Colour the pictures. Circle the correct letter.

P R J

P R B

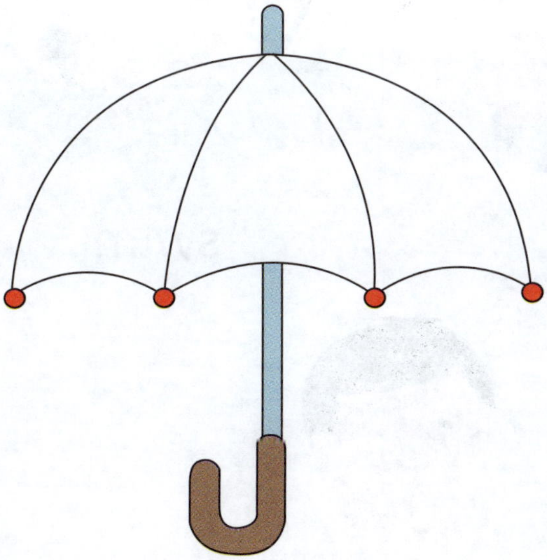

B R U

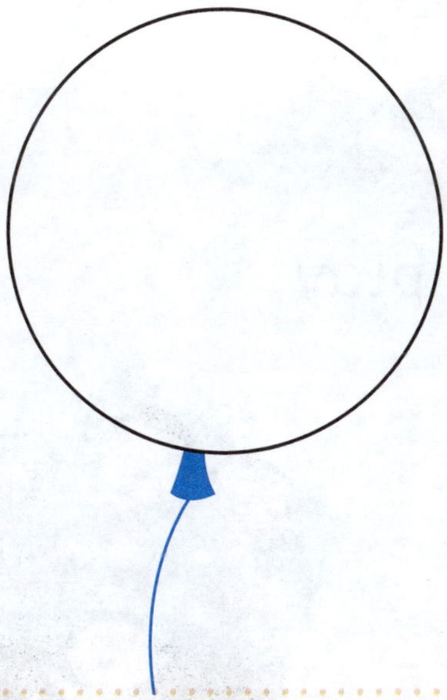

U J B

I Can!

Touch the pictures. Talk about them.

sleep

eat

drink

play

read

swim

jump

run

sit

draw

paste

climb

skate

sing

dance

paint

kick

stand

Sight Words

Touch the words. Say them loudly.

under we above

you that this

I behind

happy

she on

father he

mother

me between

Paste the correct stickers.

Hello Letter Cc

Trace with your finger. Name the pictures.

cake

carrot

cat

cup

car

cow

cap

Match the two parts of each picture.

Trace and write.

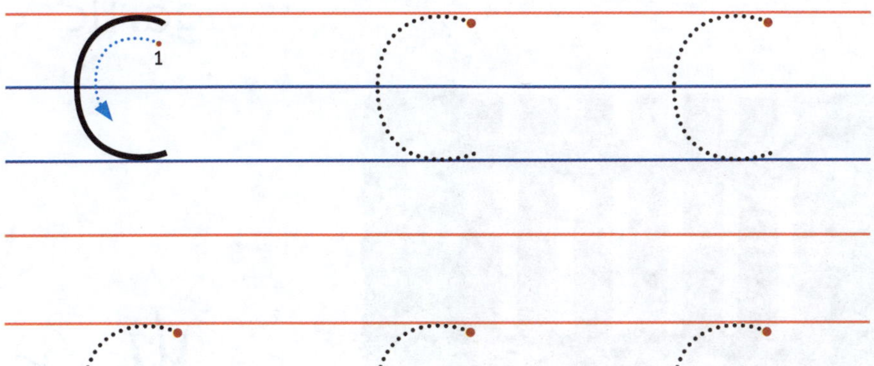

SING ALONG

Kitty cat, Kitty cat
jump to the ground.

Kitty cat, Kitty cat
don't run around.

Kitty cat, Kitty cat
catch many mice.

Kitty cat, Kitty cat
you are so nice.

Hello Letter Gg

Trace with your finger. Name the pictures.

guitar

gift

goat

garlic

girl

gate

grass

Colour the picture. Name the picture.

Trace and write.

G G G

G G G

SING ALONG

Greta goat, Greta goat,
where do you go?

Greta goat, Greta goat,
I love you so!

Greta goat, Greta goat,
stomp your feet.

Greta goat, Greta goat,
You are so sweet.

Hello Letter Dd

Trace with your finger. Name the pictures.

dog

donkey

duck

doll

dot

den

dress

Colour the dog.

Trace and write.

D

SING ALONG

Round and round,
round and round,

Dino dog runs round
and round,

Looking for his tail.

Round and round,
round and round,

Dino dog's tail is never
found,

Missing it is again!

Hello Letter Ss

Trace with your finger. Name the pictures.

snake

sink

sun

sea

sunflower

see-saw

seal

Circle the pictures that begin with S.

sunflower

doll

snake

dog

sun

Trace and write.

S S S

S S S

S

SING ALONG

Mr Sun, Mr Sun
please go away
Silky snail wants
to play.
Come again another
day!
Mr Sun, Mr Sun
please go away.

Hello Letter Oo

Trace with your finger. Name the pictures.

orange

octopus

ostrich

ox

otter

Sponge print to colour the ostrich.

Trace and write.

O

SING ALONG

Ollie ostrich, how fast
you run,
Leaving behind everyone!
Ollie ostrich, what
should I do,
So I can run as fast
as you?

Hello Letter Qq

Trace with your finger. Name the pictures.

queen

quiet

quail

quilt

quill

Match the correct pictures to Q.

Trace and write.

SING ALONG

Quincy quail, have you
any eggs?

Yes sir, yes sir,
two full kegs.

One for the market,
and one for the house,

But I have none for
greedy, grey mouse.

I Know!

Circle the correct letter.

G D S

C D O

O S Q

Q O C

G C S

S C D

Circle the correct letter.

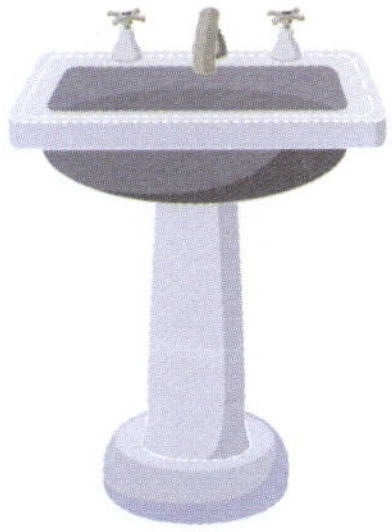

C S

D B

Q O

G C

C G

O Q

Write the matching capital letter.

s

q

d

o

g

c

I Can Write!

Trace and write.

B C D

G J O

P Q R

S U

Fun Time

Join the dots to complete the picture. Colour it.

Reading Words

Join letters to make words. Read them.

cab
dab
jab

dad
bad
lad

cap
lap
map
tap

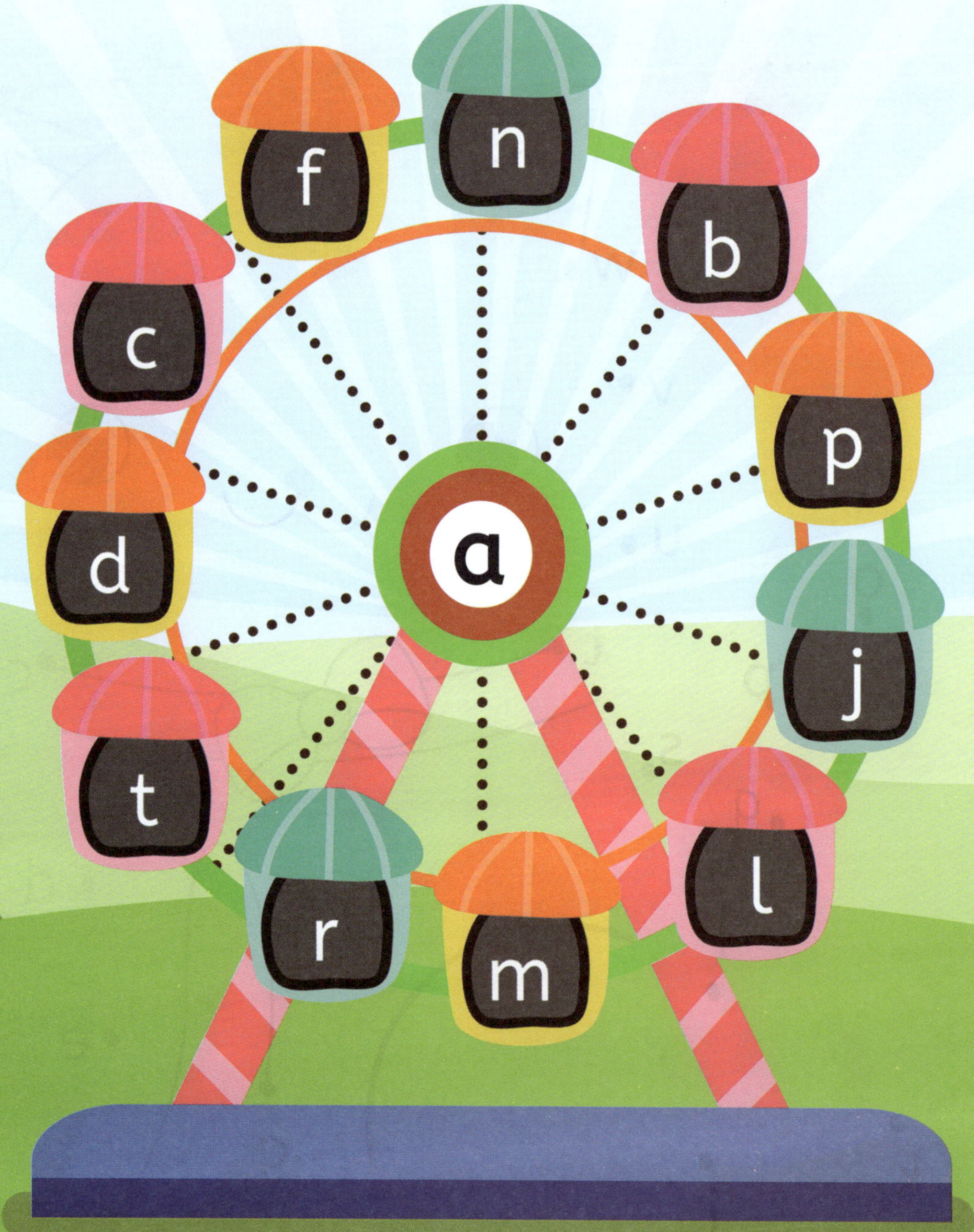

an
fan
pan
man

am
ram
dam

at
bat
cat
mat
rat

Match the pictures to the words.

map

pan

cab

rat

cat

Circle the correct word.

dad

bad

tap

map

bat

mat

fan

pan

Rhyming Words

Join letters to make words. Read them.

peg
leg

web

bet
jet
net
wet

fed
red
wed

hen
den
men
pen
ten

Match the pictures to the words.

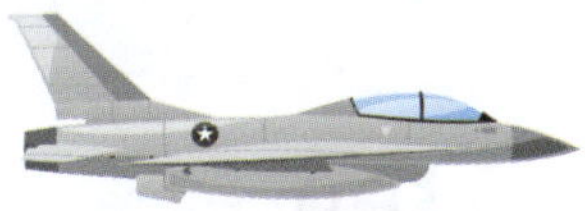

- red
- jet
- hen
- men
- den

Circle the correct word.

net

jet

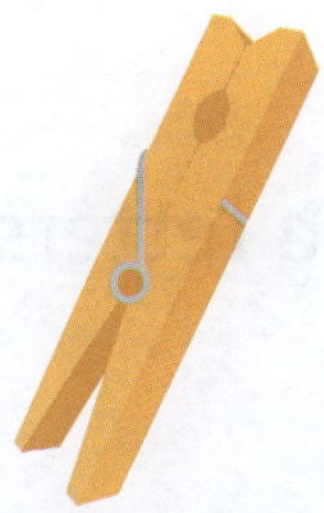

peg

leg

pen

ten

den

pen

I Can Read Words!

Cross (×) the odd one out.

cat men mat rat

hen fan men ten

pen fan man pan

jet net bat wet

Put the letters in the correct order. Read the words.

p a t

n e h

t c a

Andy Grows a Tail

Look at the pictures. Talk about them.

Listen to the story of Andy.

Reading Words

Join letters to make words. Read them.

bib
rib
nib

kid
lid
hid

in
bin
pin
tin

is
his

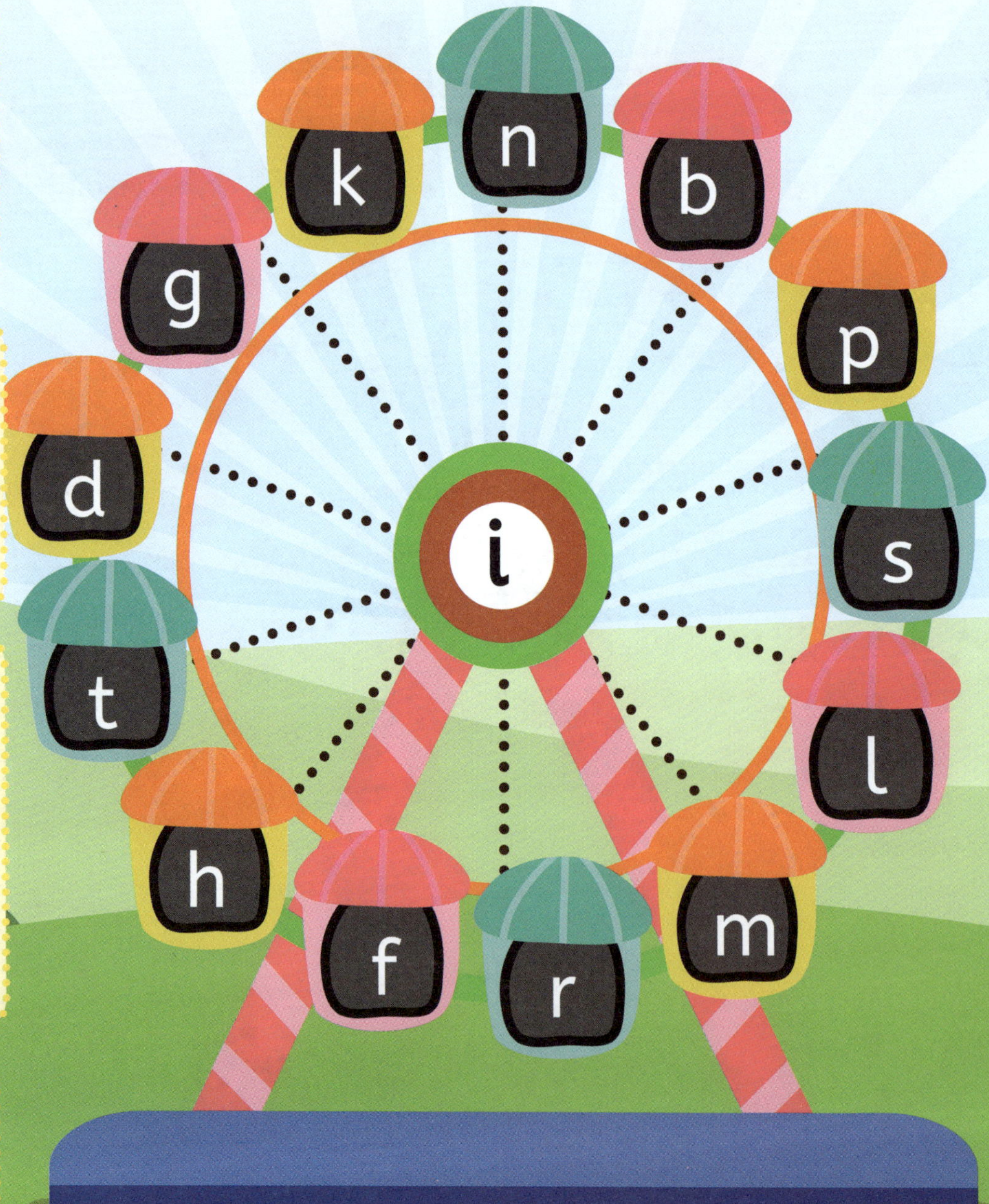

dim
him
rim

tip
sip
lip

big
fig
dig

it
bit
fit
pit

Match the pictures to the words.

- bib
- kid
- fig
- bin
- lip

Circle the correct word.

bib / rib

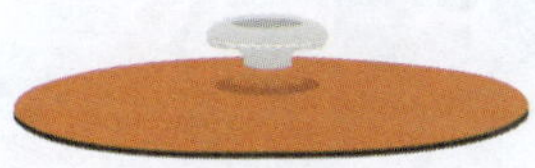

kid / lid

big / dig

tin / bin

Reading Words

Join letters to make words. Read them.

sob
rob
mob

cot
pot
hot

hop
top
pop

dog
log
fog

pod
rod
nod

Match the pictures to the words.

	sob
	dog
	pod
	pot
	hop

Circle the correct word.

rob

mob

log

fog

pot

cot

hop

top

I Can Read Words!

Cross (×) the the odd one out.

kid	pit	hid	lid
sip	pin	tin	bin
cot	pot	pod	hot
dog	mob	fog	log

Put the letters in the correct order. Read the words.

d o p

i g d

g l o

Ollie and Her Friends

Look at the pictures. Talk about them.

Listen to the story of Ollie and her friends.

Reading Words

Join letters to make words. Read them.

tub
rub

gum
up
cup

bud
mud

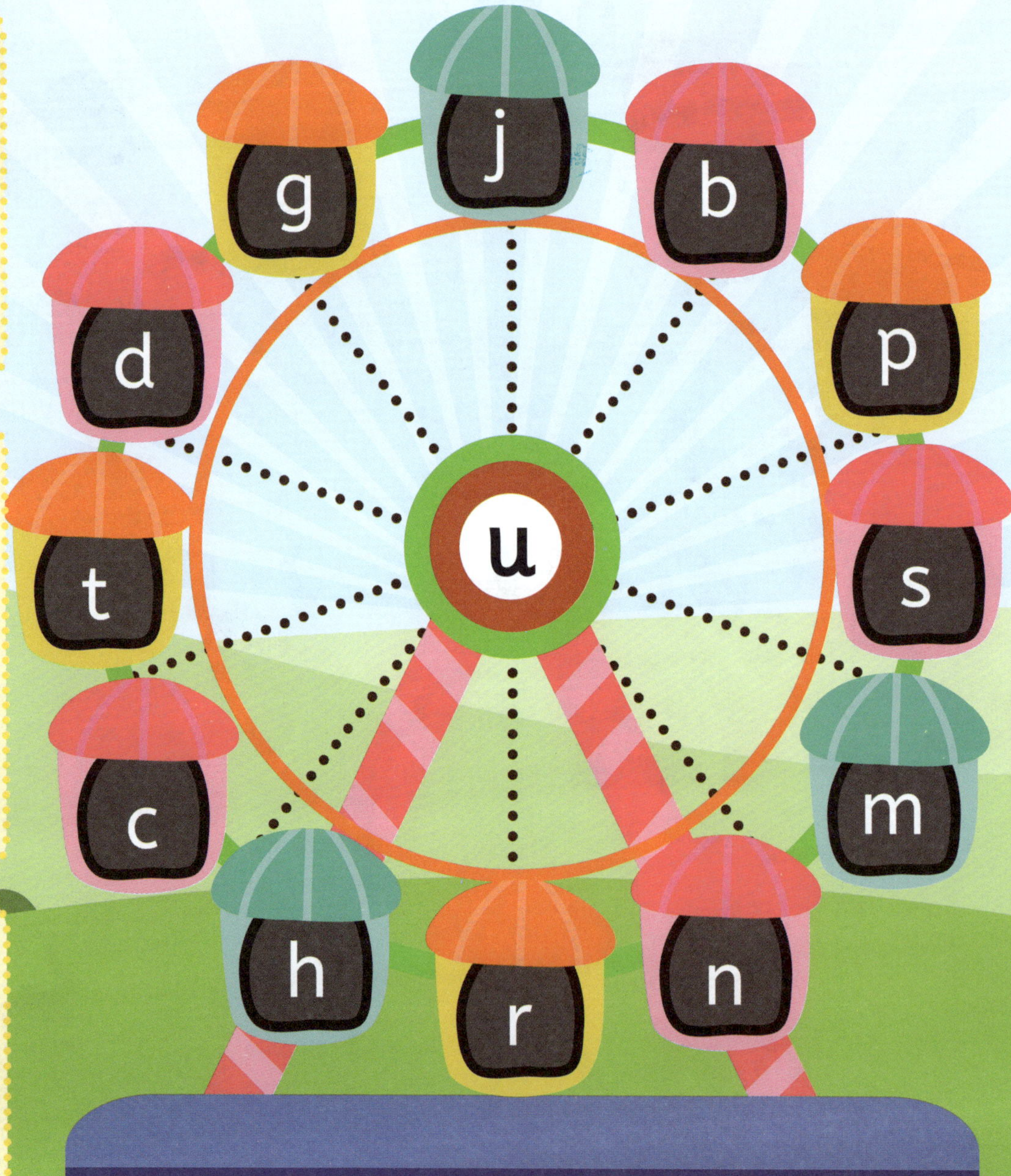

jug
bug

hut
nut

bun
run
sun

Match the pictures to the words.

tub

bud

cup

bug

hut

Circle the correct word.

tub

nut

sun

gum

bug

jug

run

bun

I Can Read Words!

Match the words to the pictures.

- cap
- jug
- pet
- sad
- pin
- mop
- hut
- net

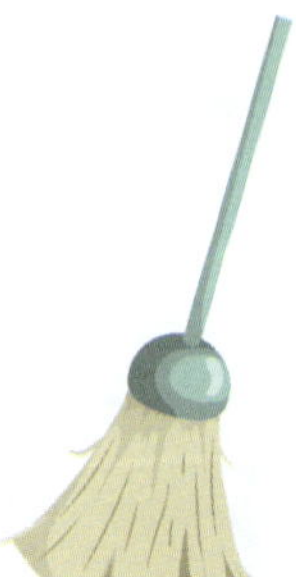

Word Bingo

Listen carefully. Cross out (×) the words that you hear.

tub	lap	dad
peg	den	hit
pit	mob	hop

Paste the correct sticker on the butterfly wings.

Tic-Tac-Toe

Play with your friends. Have fun!

Teacher's Tip:

Children can play this game in small groups, under adult supervision. Each player must close their eyes and place their finger on the outermost circle. They should move their finger on the page in circular motion to select three random letters. At least, one of the letters should be a vowel. The game can be played to reinforce letter-sounds, assess vocabulary, or even build new words.

Write the missing letters.

i

u

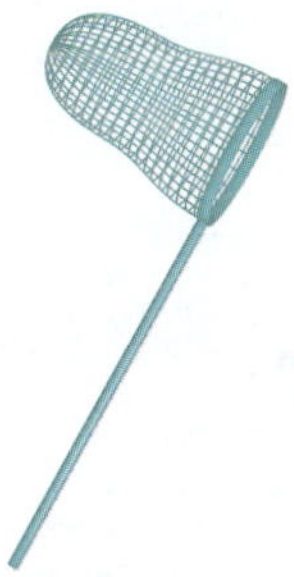

e

a

o

e

Sight Word Wall

Point and read.

from	read	mother
father	look	it
day	girl	happy
this	boy	she
of	by	that

J j U u B b R r P p

above under that I

happy you on we

father this he

she between mother

me behind

men rod rat bun big